A Consumer's Guide for Kids

A Children's Book about Buying Products and Services Wisely

by

Joy Wilt

Illustrated by Ernie Hergenroeder

Educational Products Division
Word, Incorporated
Waco, Texas

Author

JOY WILT is creator and director of Children's Ministries, an organization that provides resources "for people who care about children"—speakers, workshops, demonstrations, consulting services, and training institutes. A certified elementary school teacher, administrator, and early childhood specialist, Joy is also consultant to and professor in the master's degree program in children's ministries for Fuller Theological Seminary. Joy is a graduate of LaVerne College, LaVerne, California (B.A. in Biological Science), and Pacific Oaks College, Pasadena, California (M.A. in Human Development). She is author of three books, *Happily Ever After, An Uncomplicated Guide to Becoming a Superparent,* and *Taming the Big Bad Wolves,* as well as the popular *Can-Make-And-Do Books.* Joy's commitment "never to forget what it feels like to be a child" permeates the many innovative programs she has developed and her work as lecturer, consultant, writer, and—not least—mother of two children, Christopher and Lisa.

Artist

ERNIE HERGENROEDER is founder and owner of Hergie & Associates (a visual communications studio and advertising agency). With the establishment of this company in 1975, "Hergie" and his wife, Faith, settled in San Jose with their four children, Lynn, Kathy, Stephen, and Beth. Active in community and church affairs, Hergie is involved in presenting creative workshops for teachers, ministers, and others who wish to understand the techniques of communicating visually. He also lectures in high schools to encourage young artists toward a career in commercial art. Hergie serves as a consultant to organizations such as the Police Athletic League (PAL), Girl Scouts, and religious and secular corporations. His ultimate goal is to touch the hearts of kids (8 to 80) all over the world—visually!

ISBN: 0-8499-8138-7
Library of Congress Catalog Card Number: 79-50617
Bruce Johnson, Editor

Contents

Introduction

A Consumer's Guide for Kids is one of a series of books.   The complete set is called *Ready-Set-Grow!*

A Consumer's Guide for Kids deals with buying products and services wisely and can be used by itself or as part of a program that utilizes all of the *Ready-Set-Grow!* books.

A Consumer's Guide for Kids is specifically designed so that children can either read the book themselves or have it read to them. This can be done at home, church, or school. When reading to children, it is not necessary to complete the book at one sitting. Concern should be given to the attention span of the individual child and his or her comprehension of the subject matter.

A Consumer's Guide for Kids is designed to involve the child in the concepts that are being taught. This is done by simply and carefully explaining each concept and then asking questions that invite a response from the child. It is hoped that by answering the questions the child will personalize the concept and, thus, integrate it into his or her thinking.

Adults understand the importance of developing money responsibility, but very little has been written to explain the "push and pull" of today's economic system in terms simple enough for children to understand. Most children become consumers at an early age. These young consumers need to realize and appreciate the wise use of money in buying good products and services.

A Consumer's Guide for Kids explains how a consumer is encouraged to buy and gives three important guidelines to follow when buying:

> know the seller,
>
> know the price, and
>
> know the product or service
>
> before you spend your money.

A Consumer's Guide for Kids also contains a general disscussion of the legal rights of minors. Please note, however, that this book is not intended to replace the advice of an attorney. Neither you nor your children should rely on this book for legal advice regarding any particular transaction.

A Consumer's Guide for Kids is designed to teach a child that everything we have comes to us as a gift from God and that being a wise consumer is a part of becoming good stewards of God's gifts. Children who grow up believing and accepting this will be better equipped to live happy, fulfilling lives.

A Consumer's Guide for Kids

No matter who you are, most likely you are a consumer.

Do you know what it means to be a consumer? If you don't know what it means to be a consumer, that's OK because this book will tell you all about it.

Chapter 1

What Does It Mean to Be a Consumer?

To help you understand what a consumer is . . .

This is Susie. Susie has a lemon tree in her backyard. One day, Susie decides that she would like to make some lemonade and sell it.

To make the lemonade, Susie squeezes the juice out of the lemons and adds sugar and water.

The lemons, sugar, and water are called the <u>raw materials</u>. The lemonade is called the <u>product</u>.

To let people know about her lemonade, Susie places signs around her neighborhood. This is called <u>advertising.</u>

Susie then sets up a lemonade stand. Now Susie has a <u>firm</u> or <u>business</u>. The money that Susie spends on raw materials, advertising, and setting up her place of business is called an <u>investment</u>.

Some people come to Susie's lemonade stand and want to buy some lemonade. These people are called <u>customers</u> or <u>patrons</u>.

The amount of money that the lemonade costs the customer is called the <u>price</u>.

When someone buys a glass of lemonade, Susie makes a <u>sale</u>.

This makes Susie a <u>seller</u> and the other person a <u>consumer</u> or <u>buyer</u>.

If Susie's firm is to keep going, Susie must make enough money to pay for her <u>expenses</u>. She must earn enough money to pay for her investment in the raw materials, advertising, and the lemonade stand.

If Susie does not sell enough lemonade to pay for her expenses, she will have a <u>loss</u> and possibly go into <u>debt</u>. This means that she would owe money to someone.

Any money Susie has left after she pays her expenses is called a <u>profit</u>.

The goal of most firms is to make a profit.

Sometimes firms that try to make a profit fail. There are several reasons why this can happen.

Some firms fail to make a profit because they try to sell a product that the consumer does not need or want.

Some firms fail to make a profit because they charge more money for their product than the consumer is willing to pay.

Sometimes it is better for the consumer to buy a product from a **competitor**. A competitor is a firm that sells the same product. When a competitor sells a product for less money than another firm, it is called **underselling**.

What does all this mean?

If a firm is going to make a profit on the product it sells, there are several things it must make the consumer believe.

The seller must make the consumer believe that . . .

he or she needs or wants the product,

the price of the product is a fair price, and

the seller makes the best product, or the best place to buy the product is from this seller.

How does a seller show you, the consumer, that . . .

       you need or want the product,
       the price is right, and
       this is the place to buy?

The next chapter will tell you how.

Chapter 2

Getting the Consumer to Buy

One of the main ways a seller gets a consumer to buy is through <u>advertising</u>. The purpose of advertising is to get the attention of the consumer, make him or her know about a product, and then make him or her want to buy it.

There are many kinds of advertising.

One kind of advertising is <u>printed</u> advertising.

This includes advertisements in magazines . . .

and newspapers.

Another kind of advertising is <u>broadcast</u> advertising.

This includes advertisements on radio . . .

SUSIE'S LEMONADE IS THE
BEST IN TOWN.
IT TASTES SO GOOD
WHEN YOU DRINK IT
DOWN.

and television.

SUSIE'S LEMONADE IS THE BEST IN TOWN. IT TASTES SO GOOD WHEN YOU DRINK IT DOWN.

Radio and television advertisements are called <u>commercials</u>.

A third kind of advertising is <u>outdoor</u> advertising.

This includes signs, posters, and billboards.

Some signs and posters are put on buses, trains, taxis, and trucks.
This is called <u>transit</u> advertising.

A fourth kind of advertising is <u>direct mail</u> advertising. This includes . . .

brochures or fliers, catalogs, order forms, and
mail order ads in magazines and newspapers
for products that are ordered and delivered by mail.

There is also advertising in the <u>yellow pages</u> of the telephone book.

There are also unusual advertising <u>gimmicks</u> like skywriting, special events, and hot air balloons. Many firms use advertisements printed on ballpoint pens, shopping bags, and other giveaway novelties.

What do advertisements say? What is it about them that makes people want to buy a particular product?

Advertising is a tricky business. Often it tries to trick people into buying a product.

Here are a few of the tricks advertisers use.

MUSICAL JINGLES AND SLOGANS

These cute songs and sayings are usually fun to sing or say and easy to remember. Advertisers hope that people will think about their product every time the songs are sung or the slogans are said.

"SAVE MONEY!"

Advertisers try to make people think they can save money
if they buy the product.

ENDORSEMENTS BY FAMOUS PEOPLE

Advertisers pay famous people to endorse (say good things about) their products. Because a lot of people want to be just like famous people, advertisers hope that people will buy a product because a famous person says the product is good.

ENDORSEMENTS BY ORDINARY PEOPLE

Advertisers have ordinary people say a product is good so that other ordinary people will believe that it's true.

"JOIN THE CROWD!"

Advertisers try to get people to believe that everyone buys their product. They want you to feel left out if you don't.

Other advertising tricks are saying that . . .

      the product will cause you to be more beautiful,
      more successful, or more popular;

      the product is better than any other product like it;

      the product will make your life easier; or

      the product will make your life better, more fun,
      and exciting.

Also, advertisers sometimes use big words to make people think
that what they say about the product is scientifically true.

Advertising is one of the most effective things a seller uses to get consumers to buy. However, it is not the only thing a seller can use.

Other things a seller can use to get consumers to buy include . . .

packaging,

displays, and

bargains.

Packages are the containers in which products are sold. Sometimes a package is made to make a product look bigger than it really is. This happens when a seller uses a package that is larger than it needs to be to hold the product.

A package can also make a product look better than it really is. This is done with attractive pictures, colors, and words that are placed on the outside of the package.

A **display** is the way a product is set up to be seen in a store. Displays can also make products look better than they are.

A display can also make a person want to buy a product even when it isn't something he or she needs or wants.

A **bargain** is a product that is sold at a reduced or lower price. While it is possible to save money by buying a bargain, many people buy things they don't need or want just because the price is lower than normal.

There are several things you should know about products that are placed on sale. Pages 88—93 will tell you more about sale bargains.

As you can see, a seller will do almost anything to get the consumer to buy.

A seller will use . . .

    advertising,

    packaging,

    displays, and

    bargains to sell product.

If you're a consumer, you must be careful!

Don't believe everything you see and hear!

Find out for yourself whether or not a product is OK before you buy it.

Chapter 3

Buying Things

The first time you spend money on a product or service, you become a consumer.

As long as you continue spending money on products and services, you will continue to be a consumer.

If you are like most consumers your age, you will spend money on food, drinks . . .

toys, games, and equipment.

Like most consumers your age, you will probably spend money on recreation and entertainment.

Like most consumers your age, you may also spend money on clothes . . .

DRESSING ROOMS ➡

magazines, books, records, tapes, and school supplies.

Where do consumers your age get the products they buy?

Of course, there are all kinds of stores that sell the products children buy.

Children also send away by mail for things that are advertised in magazines, on cereal boxes, in brochures, and in catalogs.

Sometimes children buy used items from other people.
This is called buying things "secondhand."

Sometimes a salesperson will go from house to house and try to sell a product. This kind of selling is called "door-to-door" sales.

But whether you spend your money on . . .

food,
drinks,
toys,
games,
equipment,
recreation,
entertainment,
clothes,
magazines,
books,
records,
tapes, or
school supplies,

and whether you purchase things . . .

at a store,
through the mail,
secondhand, or
from a door-to-door salesperson . . .

you need to think before you spend your money!

It is a seller's goal to make a profit, but . . .

It is a consumer's goal to get his or her money's worth when buying a service or product.

The next chapter will tell you how you can reach this goal.

Chapter 4

Getting Your Money's Worth

To make sure you get your money's worth when you buy a service or product, you need to remember several things.

Avoid spending money suddenly without thinking. This is called impulse spending. Before you spend your money, ask yourself two questions.

Do I really need or want this?
Is this something I can do without?

Remember the difference between a <u>necessity</u> and a <u>luxury</u>. A necessity is something you absolutely have to have. A luxury is something you would like to have but could do without. Most of the things you purchase are probably luxuries rather than necessities.

Also, make sure that you . . .

    know the seller,
    know the price, and
    know the product or service . . .

<u>before</u> you spend your money!

To know the seller . . .   find out whether the seller sells good quality products at fair and honest prices.

You will also want to know whether the seller will give you good service.

A good seller will always try to help you get exactly what you need or want.

Find out whether the seller will stand behind his or her product. A good seller will protect the customer by not selling poor quality products. Should you buy something that doesn't work properly or isn't what you wanted, return it to the seller. A good seller will allow you to exchange the product or give you your money back.

To find out whether a certain seller is a good one, compare other sellers that have the same products.

You can also learn about a seller by talking with other people.

To know the price . . .

find out whether the price of a certain product is a fair and honest price.

You will want to compare prices by looking through newspapers, magazines, and catalogs; and calling or visiting different stores.

You might also talk to people who have purchased the product. Find out where they bought the product and how much they paid for it.

You may be fortunate enough to find the product you want on sale. This means the product now costs less money than it usually does.

But be careful when you buy a product on sale. You are taking a risk. Do you know why this is true?

Most often, you won't be allowed to exchange or get a cash refund on an item bought on sale.

In addition, you may find that sale items are often . . .

<u>As is</u> — The product is missing parts or has been chipped, torn, or broken.

<u>Seconds</u> — The product is not the best quality possible.

<u>Irregulars</u> — The product has some flaws or imperfections in it.

<u>Special purchases</u> — The product has been purchased in a large quantity. It is likely that many people will own identical items.

You may also find that sale items are often . . .

<u>Out of style</u> — The product (usually clothes) is no longer in fashion.

<u>Out of season</u> — The product is not usable now because the time to use the product has already passed. You may have to wait several months before you will be able to use an out of season product.

<u>Obsolete</u> — The product is no longer made. It may be impossible to replace broken parts or have it repaired. There may also be a new, improved model that works better than the old one.

Not all sale products will be . . .

as is,
seconds,
irregulars,
special purchases,
out of style,
out of season, or
obsolete.

But, it's up to you to find out why an item is on sale.

You should examine a product carefully before you buy it.

Buying a product on sale can save you money, but only if you use it and it does what you expect it to do.

To know the product . . .

Look each and every product over carefully before you buy it.

If you are buying packaged food or drinks, read the labels.

Find out if the product contains anything you don't like or that could harm you.

Also, check the amount you are getting. Sometimes packages fool you into thinking you are getting more of the product than you really are.

If you are buying prepared food and drinks somewhere, ask the seller what is in the product you want to buy and exactly how much you will get.

Don't buy products from a seller who is not willing to give you this information.

If you are buying a toy, game, or piece of equipment, make sure it is safe.

See that it doesn't have sharp points or edges, pinch places like springs or hinges, small parts that could be swallowed by a younger child, or rough places that could scrape or cut you.

Try to buy items that can be cleaned, won't burn easily, won't cause allergies, or aren't poisonous.

If you buy a toy, game, or piece of equipment, you might want to ask yourself these questions.

Can I use the item in more than one way?

How long will the item last? Is it built to take normal wear when it is used?

Will the item work? Does it have all of its parts? Will it do what it is supposed to do?

Can I use the item on my own, or will I need a lot of help from an adult?

Is the item attractive to me? Is it something I would really want?

Am I old enough and skilled enough to use the item?

If you spend money on entertainment
or recreation, make sure it . . .

is something your parents approve of, is suitable for children your age, will have a good effect on you, and is something you will appreciate and enjoy.

If you spend money on clothes, make sure you get ones you will feel good about wearing. Get someone to help you pick out things that will last.

Always read the label before you buy anything.

Find out what will have to be done to clean and take care of the item. It is best if the item can be washed in a machine. Remember that dry cleaning is expensive and washing clothes by hand is a bother.

Make sure the clothes fit you and are made well.

If you have any questions, it is a good idea to ask a person who knows about clothes to help you decide whether the item would be a wise purchase.

If you spend money on magazines, books, records, or tapes, make sure they . . .

are ones your parents approve of,
are suitable for children your age,
will have a good effect on you, and
are ones you can understand and enjoy.

Also, you should try to select a variety of magazines, books, records, and tapes.

Here is a list to help you pick out the different kinds that are available.

<u>FANTASY</u> — These have fun stories, songs, and activities that stimulate and exercise your imagination.

<u>TECHNIQUE</u> — These show you how to make or do things.

<u>PARTICIPATION</u> — These offer word games, puzzles, pictures to draw or color, and other activities for you to do.

<u>ACADEMIC</u> — These teach you things like social studies, science, and nature, and also help you with your reading, writing, and math skills.

<u>AFFIRMATIONAL</u> — These help you gain an understanding and appreciation of yourself and the people around you.

<u>INSPIRATIONAL</u>
<u>AND RELIGIOUS</u> — These help you understand religion and spiritual things. They encourage you to become a better person.

If you think before you spend your money, you will get your money's worth most of the time.

However, once in a while you might not get what you pay for. The next chapter will tell you what to do when this happens.

Chapter 5

What to Do When You Don't Get What You Pay For

Suppose you buy a product, take it home, and . . .   it is too easily broken
or destroyed,
it doesn't work properly,
it doesn't fit properly,
or it isn't what
you thought it was.

Or suppose you change your mind and do not want what you purchased.

What can you do about it?

To start with, when you purchase anything, there are four things you should be sure to keep.

SALES RECEIPT — This is the piece of paper that comes from the cash register or is written by the seller. It tells what you bought and how much you paid for it.

TAGS — These are the pieces of paper, cardboard, or plastic that are attached to a product. These tell about the product, who made it, and how much it costs.

SALES RECEIPT   TAGS

CONTAINER — This is the box, plastic bag, or other material the product came in when it was bought.

GUARANTY or **WARRANTY** — This is a written promise about the quality of the product. Often the buyer is promised his or her money back if the product does not do what it should.

CONTAINER

GUARANTY OR
WARRANTY

Keep the sales receipt, tags, and container until you are sure you won't decide to return the product.

Keep the guaranty or warranty until the time in which it can be used runs out. Most are good for 30 days, 90 days, or sometimes longer.

If you choose to return a product, take it along with the sales receipt, tags, container, and guaranty back to where you purchased the product.

Go to the customer service department or the manager of the store. Tell the customer service representative or the manager kindly and honestly why you want to return the product.

If you return the product in a reasonable amount of time,
if you have a good reason for returning the product, and
if you are kind about returning it . . .

chances are the customer service representative or the manager will be
willing to make an exchange or give your money back.

If the seller will not let you return the product, ask your parents to help you. The law is in your favor.

The law states that a <u>minor</u> may <u>void</u> almost any <u>contract</u> he or she makes.

A minor is a person below a certain age who is under his or her parents' guidance. Depending on state laws, most states say a minor is a person under 18 or 21 years old.

Void means to cancel or to make of no value.

A contract is an agreement between two or more people.

One thing this means is that if you bought something and then decided to return it, the person who sold you the product must refund your money.

It also means that if you sell something to someone and then decide you want it back, the person who bought the item from you must give it back if you return his or her money.

The law protects young people from being hurt by an unwise agreement. Although this is true, this does not mean that you should make careless decisions.

If you want people to trust and respect you, you must be a person that is worthy of trust and respect. This means that you should never enter into a contract or agreement with another person unless you intend to keep your part of the deal.

Here is another way the law protects you.

Suppose you get something in the mail you didn't ask to be sent to you. This is called <u>unsolicited mail</u>. If this happens, there are several things you can do.

Perhaps the best thing you can do is to . . .

not open the package,

write "Refused" or "Return to Sender" on the front of it, and

mail it back to the sender.

If you leave the package unopened, you should not have to pay anything to return it to the sender. If you open the package, you will have to pay the postage or shipping charge to return it.

If you open the package and feel you don't want to pay to return it, set it aside for a reasonable amount of time. If it is not claimed by the sender, you may do whatever you wish with it.

You do not have to pay for anything that you did not ask to be sent to you.

If you should ever send away for something, there are two important things you should always remember.

Never send cash through the mail. Use a check or a money order instead.

Order products only from a seller you know you can trust.

Suppose you send away for something and never receive it. If you didn't send any money, you will have lost nothing. But if you did send money, there are several things you should do.

First, you should always save a copy of the order form or letter that you sent to ask for the product. Keep your money order receipt or watch for the canceled check to return. Also keep any brochures, pamphlets, or anything else used to advertise the product.

Wait six to eight weeks. If the product hasn't come by that time . . .

Call or write the seller from which you ordered the product. Ask if your order was received and when the product will be sent.

If the seller received your order and your money but refuses to send you the product, go to your local post office and ask for help. Be sure to take the copy of your order form or letter and your canceled check or money order receipt.

Conclusion

Because you spend money on products and services, you are a consumer.
You will probably continue to be a consumer all of your life.

To be a smart consumer, remember these things.

> Don't believe everything you see and hear through advertising, packaging, displays, and bargain gimmicks.

> Know the seller, know the price, and know the product or service before you spend your money.

> If you decide to return a product, do it in a reasonable amount of time, and do it kindly.

Remember, being a consumer can be fun and exciting as long as you . . .

Get your money's worth when you buy a service or product!